Made in Illinois

AN ARTISAN GALLERY

Portrait and Artwork Photography by
David Wagenaar

Landscape and Tourism Photography by
the Illinois Department of Commerce and
Community Affairs, Bureau of Tourism,
Jason Lindsey, and Robert Shaw

Writer
Glenn Gordon

Book Design
Nicholas Associates/Chicago

First Edition

Cover Photograph
Sorrel and Native Grasses
on an Illinois Sand Prairie

Printed by the Authority of the State of Illinois
209387

200M 2/01

Prologue

Early in the spring of 2000, at the invitation of First Lady Lura Lynn Ryan, representatives of the Illinois Department of Commerce and Community Affairs, Illinois Arts Council, Capital Development Board, Department of Natural Resources, Illinois Artisans Program, Illinois State Museum and Office of the Governor came together to develop a unique catalogue designed to highlight the artisans of Illinois. The goal of this group was to produce a book, titled *Made in Illinois*, that would identify Illinois artisans, illustrate their art work, and demonstrate the excellence and diversity of the crafts of this state. The greatest challenge to this group was to seek out the highest quality work while ensuring that every artisan in the state had the opportunity to be considered. To that end, a multi-level jury process was established to identify artists and encourage their involvement. The first phase involved nominations from museum directors from Northern, Eastern, Western, Central, and Southern Illinois. The second phase involved an open competition announced in newspapers throughout the state. As a result of these two methods, hundreds of Illinois artisans working in glass, clay, fibers, metal and a variety of other materials had their artwork reviewed by seven art professionals representing every area of the state. To the delight of the jury, a great number of outstanding artisans emerged from each phase of the process. With state museum-operated galleries and artisan shops at the James R. Thompson Center in Chicago, Illinois State Museum in Springfield and Rend Lake Artisan Shop, in Southern Illinois, the state has made a commitment to support the artisans of Illinois. This publication, however, was designed to present the high level of handmade crafts in Illinois to an even greater audience. At the same time, the book would illustrate the state's wide variety of terrain and natural features that serve not only as a home, but also as a source of inspiration to these artists.

By bringing these locations and artists together in one publication, this book can be used to chart destinations for the best in crafts as well as locations of interest. To serve that purpose, the publication has been divided into three districts: Northern, Central and Southern Illinois, with listings of artisans from each district. As *Made in Illinois* came together it was obvious that Illinois is a state rich in cultural resources. Of equal importance is the number of fine individuals who realize the significance of these resources. Thanks to Shirley Madigan, Rhoda Pierce, Susan Cavanaugh, Nita Crews, Desi Harris, Kim Robinson, Estie Karpman, and Ellen Gantner for their efforts in making the concept of this publication a reality. There are two people for whom this project went beyond a labor of love and without whom this publication could not have taken place. The first truly loves the arts and has taken every opportunity to promote this concept since her husband was Lt. Governor in 1983—Illinois' First Lady, Lura Lynn Ryan. The second has an equal passion for the arts, and understands the significance of cultural tourism and its impact on the state economy—Pam McDonough, Director of the Illinois Department of Commerce and Community Affairs. For me, it has been an honor to serve with these dedicated individuals on this project. As *Made in Illinois* was being assembled, it was a pleasure to see so many of my favorite Illinois locations serve as the backdrop for the fine crafts of this state. My greatest pleasure however, was to see so many outstanding artisans of Illinois recognized in this publication.

Michael A. Dunbar
Coordinator, Art in Architecture
Illinois Capital Development Board

CONTENTS

Illinois' Artisan Treasures

It is with great pleasure and pride that I join the Illinois Department of Commerce and Community Affairs in presenting this gallery of the work of our state's finest artisans. The creativity of our craftspeople infuses every corner of Illinois with economic and cultural vitality. From the river towns and busy cities of the north, through the rich wide farmland of the central region, to the rolling hills and forests of the south, our artisans are transforming the age-old materials of clay, fiber, metal, paper, leather, wood, and glass, into bowls, cups, jewelry, lamps, baskets, quilts, rugs, tools, and works of furniture that will surely last for generations. We encourage all who wish to see more of the work of Illinois artisans to seek them out through the directory in the back of this book and visit the regions where they live. As you'll see in the preludes to each region in the book, Illinois is rich with historic and scenic sites, cultural festivals, and great outdoor recreational destinations. The wonder and beauty of Illinois has inspired these artists and has served as a perfect backdrop for their

First Lady Lura Lynn Ryan at the Artisan Tent at the Illinois State Fair.

work—exceptional work in an exceptional state. Many of this book's artists are participants in the Artisans Program of the Illinois State Museum. Their works are often on exhibit and for sale in the Program's Artisans Shops in Chicago and Rend Lake and in the State Museum's gift shops in Springfield and Dickson Mounds, all of which we cordially invite you to visit—we promise you will not be disappointed. A work created by hand is different than something that comes off a factory's conveyor belt. A work of craft is imprinted with the touch of an individual human being. It seems the more old skills die away, the more we hunger for evidence that those skills–the knowledge of how to weave a shawl, throw a pot, dovetail a drawer—still exist. For all the astonishments of technology, the hand is still the most amazing tool of all, and the work done by the people in this book is proof of it.

Lura Lynn Ryan

Lura Lynn Ryan

Northern
Illinois

ast to west, from the annual international exhibitions of outdoor sculpture on the windy lakefront of

Chicago to the Arts District of Rock Island on the banks of the Mississippi River, the northern region

of Illinois abounds in cultural activity. One could spend months in the museums of Chicago alone, the

Art Institute, the Field Museum, the Museum of Contemporary Art, the Shedd Aquarium, the Adler Planetarium,

the Museum of Science and Industry—the list could go on. Ten miles west of the Loop and its phenomenal

works of architecture such as the Harold Washington Public Library, the Sears Tower and the John Hancock

Building, is the Frank Lloyd Wright Historic District in Oak Park, with the largest concentration of the master's

Prairie Style houses to be found anywhere. If you like Wright, you must also see the Robie House, near the cam-

pus of the University of Chicago, in Hyde Park. Further afield, and a spectacular reason to spend the day outdoors,

is the bucolic Morton Arboretum, which features 1500 acres of the best in botany. Also within an hour's reach of

Chicago to the north are the sculpture gardens of Northwestern University in Evanston and south of the city at

Governor's State University. For a respite from all the cultural intensity, give yourself time for a stay at Starved

Rock State Park, whose main lodge is one of Illinois' noblest monuments to the workmanship of the WPA, with

good food to boot. Another fascinating place to tour not far outside the city is the Fermilab in Batavia, a mecca

of experimental physics, where a herd of buffalo grazes in the fields above one of the world's largest

underground particle accelerators. Nearby is the flyway and bird sanctuary of the Fox River. From there, one can

drive across the state to the palisades and wildlife refuges of the Mississippi and up the Great River Road through

lovely rolling hills and farmland to the galleries, antique and crafts shops of the pretty town of Galena.

Left
Lake Michigan at Illinois Beach State Park, Zion

Akiko
Koiso
MOLINE

Using techniques from the raku tradition of her native Japan, Akiko Koiso explores a great range of ideas in ceramic sculpture. A signature characteristic of her work is a greyish white crackle glaze with parts of the ceramics painted matte black after firing. These include constructed vessels with details of wood and twine, exquisitely symmetrical and architectural in feeling. In another series, wheel-thrown pots are carved with frogs and bamboo. More abstract are pieces called "Offerings," one of these a powerful tusk-like form captured in a scaffolding of lashed-together sticks. Other works incorporate graphics and collage. Add to this Akiko's delicately modeled sculptures of women, done with great sensitivity. "I feel peaceful when I work with clay," says Akiko, and the faces of her women show it.

Above
Untitled Raku Ceramic Sculpture with Crackled Glaze
17" x 14" x 6-1/2"

Left
Untitled Ceramic Slab Built Sculpture Painted and Airbrushed with Underglaze
22" x 17" x 8-1/2"

Above
Picasso Statue, Chicago

Left Top
Galena River Near Entrance to Downtown Galena

Left
Chicago River, Chicago

Untitled Woven Fiber Sculpture 84" x 66" x 24"

ll I need is a wall," says Dorothy Hughes, whose large fiber sculptures hang from most of the available walls of her studio in Chicago. Hughes doesn't see herself as a weaver but as a sculptor whose main tool happens to be the loom. Most of her works start out as coarse, heavy, linen and sisal yarns which she dyes herself. Her old four-harness loom was originally built for the weavers employed by the Works Progress Administration in the thirties and still bears the marking, "WPA," on its post. All of Hughes' work in fiber, ceramics, and jewelry reflects the muted organic forms and colors of the natural environment: "What's outside has to be inside…instinct and intuition are the forces that move me. I wouldn't know how to make a hard-edged, bright-colored geometric piece if my life depended on it."

Dorothy
Hughes
CHICAGO

11

Laura Wasilowski, *Elgin*
Blue Ladder Fiber 41" x 52"

Robert Sjostrom, *Rockford*
Covered Bridge, Princeton, IL Ceramics & Photography 13" Diameter

Water Lilies Cover Lake Defiance Moraine Hills State Park, McHenry

Richard Kowal, *Chicago*
Small Fish Woodworking 6-1/2" Long

Michele A. Friedman, *Chicago*
Leaf Brooch Jewelry 2-3/4" x 1-1/8"

The Whisper Earthenware with Commercial Glazes 24" x 4" x 4"

ori Roderick's painted ceramic sculptures of women, like Ms. Roderick herself, are tall and slender. The figures have niches carved into their gowns, filled with images of symbolic meaning. In "Whisper," for example, the feather is a rumor making its way to the figure's ear (via a dotted line signifying invisibility like dotted lines do in drafting.) In another niche, a tableau represents Roderick's husband and their two little boys. The niches are chapters in the narrative of Roderick's life as a mother, a wife, and—as is evident from one sculpture—a reader of a great many bedtime stories. Influenced by southwestern and Mexican primitive storytelling sculpture, Roderick says that "Primitive art, to me, is closer to life and death...there is exuberance in the way it's made—its vitality inspires me."

Lori
Roderick
ROCK ISLAND

14

Salad Bowl Hand-cut Crystal 10" Diameter

urt Strobach traces his family's lineage of crystal glass cutters and engravers back to his great-grandfathers in Bohemia. Before his emigration to the U.S., and within the span of his own memory, the lathes that spun the big sandstone wheels used to grind the glass were still powered by oxen. Strobach's showroom and house in Crystal Lake contain a brilliantly lit display of his cut vases, wine glasses, decanters, bowls, paperweights, and melodious crystal bells. Downstairs in his basement shop, Strobach inks his patterns onto pieces of plain crystal, then grinds with an array of wheels whose profiles each impart a different shape of cut. He works entirely freehand, presenting a crystal bowl to the wheel with no support other than a padded plank to brace his elbows and a pair of very steady hands.

Kurt Strobach

CRYSTAL LAKE

D. Andrew Kates, *North Aurora*
Shaker Tall Clock Wood 87" × 18" × 8-1/2"

Top
Adair Karlin, *Highland Park*
Primitif Painted Maplewood Bowl 15" Diameter

Jane A. Sassaman, *Chicago*
Tree of Life-Spring Fiber/Wall Quilt 70" × 80"

Spencer Watson, *Prospect Heights*
United Sand-blasted Lake Stones 6" × 2"

he luminous jewel-tones of Jennifer Forman Weinstein's limited edition hand-painted silk scarves created for the Chicago Lyric Opera season of 1993 were outlined to suggest a window of stained glass, an effect heightened when the scarf is held up to the light. Embedded in the design were the almost hidden letters of the words "Lyric Opera." The edition sold out almost immediately. Many of Jennifer's scarf designs originate from her work as an easel painter, the ideas evolving from canvas into silk. She has also exhibited as a sculptor and designer in a variety of other media: everything from jewelry in crystal to hypnotic works of furniture covered with holograms of blinking eyes to life-sized bronze sculptures of playful, multi-national children representing world peace.

Jennifer Forman Weinstein

CHICAGO

Top
Kaleidoscope Hand Painted Silk 15" × 60"

Bottom
New York and the Statue of Liberty Hand Painted Silk 15" × 60"

17

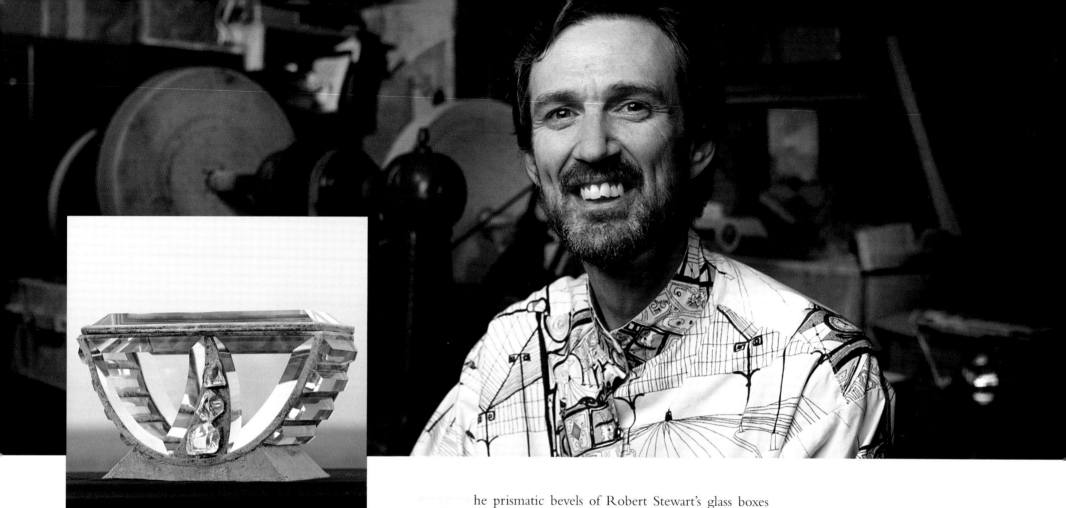

Wish Box Glass and Metal 12" x 12" x 12"

he prismatic bevels of Robert Stewart's glass boxes refract a window's light and project its rainbows to a wall twenty feet away. The art of hand beveling thick plate glass was nearly lost until Stewart conceived a passion to keep it alive. He had to hunt down the machinery he needed in the basements of old glass companies in Chicago, equipment which includes a glass lathe from Germany, a grinding wheel made of a special sandstone last mined in Newcastle England in 1945, and buffing and polishing wheels of Portuguese cork and Spanish felt. Stewart's boxes have been presented as gifts from the people of Illinois to many foreign heads of state. He made the presentation box for the Bowie knife given to former President George H.W. Bush, and the little glass igloo ornament that graces the White House Christmas tree.

Robert
Stewart
CARY

Lisa
Mahar
ROCK ISLAND

People throw out old furniture as junk. Lisa Mahar, a consummate recycler, throws the process into reverse, rescuing old chairs and tables from alleys, flea markets and garage sales, and transforming them with color into art. Other flotsam and jetsam gets into the mix too—beads, mosaic tile, vinyl fringe, papier mache, old jewelry, bits of tin and rope, and toy plastic cowboys, Indians, and frogs. A pair of high heels are used as ornamental brackets on her side table, "Tip-Tap Kitty Kat," which is painted all over with cats in zoot suits. The rim of her "Queen Table" is trimmed with colored buttons, while her "Circus Bowl Table," made of an old wood salad bowl, is covered with a lid that flips up to reveal a three ring circus inside like the one that seems to go on non-stop in Mahar's imagination.

Little Red House Chair Mixed Media/Hand-painted Furniture
35-1/2" x 17" x 17"

Michael Devlin, *Chicago*
Hour Glass Armoire Zebra Wood, Rift Sawn Ash
and Ebonized Walnut 90" x 66" x 26"

Susan Etcoff Fraerman, *Highland Park*
Lotus Shoes Off-loom Bead Weaving, Glass Beads, Found Objects, Wood, Felt, Nylon
Thread 7-3/4" x 5" x 2-3/4"

Cougar #1 Hand-painted Turkey Feather 10" x 20"

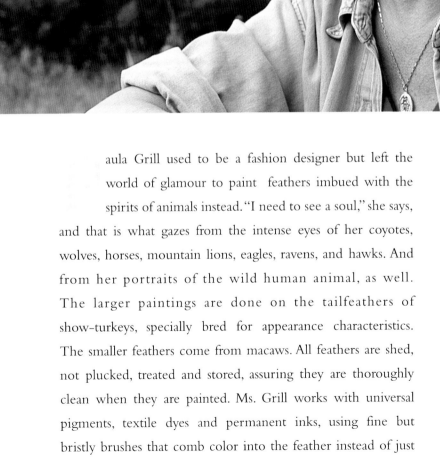

aula Grill used to be a fashion designer but left the world of glamour to paint feathers imbued with the spirits of animals instead. "I need to see a soul," she says, and that is what gazes from the intense eyes of her coyotes, wolves, horses, mountain lions, eagles, ravens, and hawks. And from her portraits of the wild human animal, as well. The larger paintings are done on the tailfeathers of show-turkeys, specially bred for appearance characteristics. The smaller feathers come from macaws. All feathers are shed, not plucked, treated and stored, assuring they are thoroughly clean when they are painted. Ms. Grill works with universal pigments, textile dyes and permanent inks, using fine but bristly brushes that comb color into the feather instead of just laying it on top.

Paula
Grill
WILMINGTON

21

Left Top
Fox River at Silver Springs State Park, Yorkville

Left
Evanston Lighthouse, Evanston

Above
Ice Falls in Wildcat Canyon at Starved Rock State Park, Utica

Feeding a Celtic Galaxy with Dark Matter Glass Panel 78" x 30"

o walk through the door of Angarola's stained glass studio is to step into a swirling cosmos of color, light, and grand opera. The voice of Luciano Pavarotti pours forth from a boombox overlooking worktables covered with the myriad colored glass fragments of works in progress. Suspended in panels in the studio's front window are several of Angarola's masterworks, one composed of Celtic knots, symbolic of planets, with hundreds of stars spiraling through the darkness of the black glass surrounding them; another the purple and cobalt "Nessum Dorma" ("No One Sleeps") named after the Puccini aria Pavarotti is singing. Nearby hangs one of the loveliest stained glass lamps you'll ever find, a lyric garden of color in the shape of a tulip. Angarola goes by his last name. His dog Bob answers to his first.

Angarola
VERNON HILLS

Elaine Unzicker, *Chicago*
Dance of the Nile Collar Stainless Steel, Bronze, Sterling Clasp
16" Diameter

Bonnie Peterson, *Elmhurst*
When I Saw Winter Heat Transfer and Embroidery on Satin Velvet and Sheers
56" x 50"

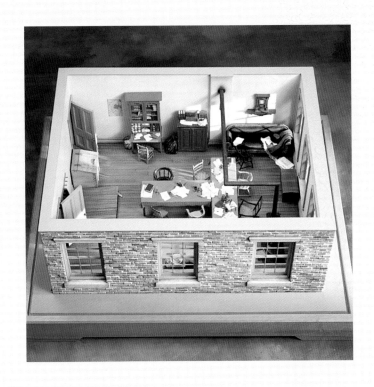

Allison Ashby & Steve Jedd, *Riverside*
Lincoln-Herndon Law Office Springfield, IL 1843-1847
1/12" Scale, Mixed Media 26" x 20" x 10"

Lincoln-Herndon Law Office Springfield, IL 1843-1847 Detail

Left Top
Navy Pier, Chicago

Left
The District, Rock Island

Above
Black Hawk Statue in Lowden State Park, Oregon

Right
Rock River at Castle Rock State Park, Oregon

Ana Buzancic Petercic, *Lincolnwood*
Cape Fiber 55" x 76"

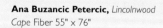

Top
Kathleen Weir-West, *Barrington*
Woven Jacket Cotton/Rayon Available Sizes 2-16

Leonard & Carolyn Wilson, *McHenry*
Three Door/Drawer Glass 6" x 8" x 2"

Top
George Weissler, *Evanston*
Celtic Bird Knot Hand Carved Mahogany 10-1/2" x 11-1/2"

Doris Sikorsky, *Chicago*
Flowers-Kwaity Cut Paper - Wycinanki 10" x 15"

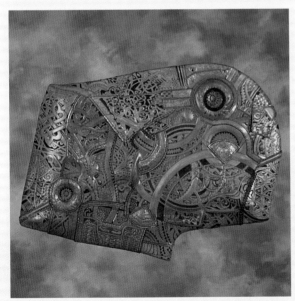

Top
Mary Watson, *Prospect Heights*
Jubilant Pins Silver, Gold, Pearl, Semi-Precious and Lake Stone 3" × 4"

Robert Gadomski, *Homewood*
The Big Bang Leather Relief 31" × 24" × 3"

Top
Ruth Weiner, *Evanston*
Buelah Sawdust Fired Stoneware Ceramic 28" × 14" Diameter

Joyce P. Lopez, *Chicago*
Quiet in Red Steel and French Cotton Thread Sculpture 31" × 31" × 1"

Marvin & Michelle Shafer, *Chicago*
Hotter or Caulder Sculpture 27" × 34"

Release of the Spirit Ceramic, Stains, and Oxides 108" x 36" x 12"

he ceramic sculptor Indira Johnson is creating a series of seated Buddhas whose upper bodies are made of found industrial objects. In "Balance of Power," Johnson uses an automobile spring and a large, halo-like ring-gear for the head. In "1-800-NIRVANA," the head is a telephone; in "Truth Seeker," a magnifying glass; in "Communication Gap," the insulator from a telephone pole. Among the prolific Johnson's other works is one made up of clipped-out marriage ads from Bombay newspapers, each ad held down by a little stone. Challenging traditional valuations of "women's worth" both in her native Bombay and here in this country, Johnson involves herself in women's economic self-determination projects, designing textiles and clothing which co-ops of women in India's villages produce for export to the West.

Indira
Freitas Johnson
E V A N S T O N

Alan Barbick, Warrenville
The Shamans Hand-carved Stone 21" x 13" x 3/4"

Karen Ovington, *Chicago*
Untitled Jewelry 60" Long

Foggy Morning on the Kankakee River at Kankakee River State Park, Bradley/Bourbonnais

Vera Samycia, *Chicago*
Pysankas - Ukranian Easter Eggs

Karla Witukiewicz, *Chicago*
Miracles of Life Sterling Silver and Antique Button Bracelet 8" × 1"

Early Ride Cast Glass 16" x 40" x 1"

Mark Fowler

ROCK ISLAND

asting sculpture in glass calls for patience," says Mark Fowler, who in recent years has been involved in design collaborations casting glass at architectural scale. "Where glassblowing is the essence of immediacy, casting is the opposite—there is always a prolonged period of waiting for the piece to mold to form, then more waiting as it is annealed in the kiln. I feel most in touch with this method, balancing the impulsive nature of glassblowing with the more deliberate steps of the casting process, which is akin to fishing. I hated fishing as a kid but love it now—for exactly the same reason: it's slow and often boring, but now it's a welcome escape from the manic pace of our lives. Casting glass or casting for trout, the sudden flashes of their intense, abstract color and pattern are inspiring."

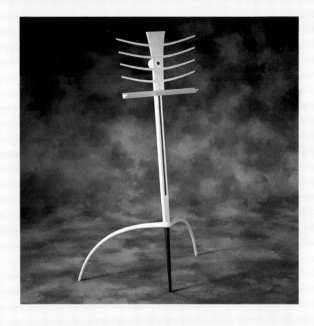

Mary Carolyn Obodzinski, *Crystal Lake*
Relic #1 Ceramics 7" × 17-1/2" × 3-1/2"

Marcia Karlin, *Lincolnshire*
Blue Garden III Fiber 63-1/2" × 39"

R. Thomas Tedrowe Jr., *Chicago*
Adjustable Music Stand Bleached Ash & Steel 50-1/2" × 29" × 15"

Above
Rectangular Tray/Oval Cups Slip Cast Red Stoneware with Glazed
and Unglazed Surfaces 3" x 16" x 6", 4-1/2" x 5" x 3"

Left
Teapot and Cups Slip Cast Red Stoneware with Glazed
and Unglazed Surfaces 5-1/2" x 8-1/2", 3' x 2-1/2" x 2-1/2"

Far Left Top
Volo Bog State Natural Area, Ingleside

Far Left Center
Blacksmith Shop, John Deere Historic Site at Grand Detour

Far Left Bottom
Front of Starved Rock Lodge at Starved Rock State Park, Utica

have always been drawn to the functional object. I seek the age-old marriage of elegant function and visually interesting form." Every piece of Paul Eshelman's slip-cast stoneware is a manifestation of that quest and a meditation on the critical questions Eshelman put to himself early in his career in clay: "What kind of stance or posture does the piece have in space? Does its surface explain, ignore, or negate the form? How does this piece work for us? How does it treat us? If it is meant to function, does it? Does it appear kind or scornful? Are its pronouncements spoken in a language we can comprehend?" Eshelman's works speak well for themselves. They are dishwasher and microwave-safe. Their contrasting unglazed areas are non-porous and absorb no liquid, and the glazes are subtle and harmonious.

Paul Eshelman
ELIZABETH

Larry Zgoda, *Chicago*
Butterflies Stained Glass 40" x 20"

Deborah Shank, *Northbrook*
10" Fibonacci Twill Basket 21 Woodworking 10" x 4"

Weeks Ringle and Bill Kerr, *Oak Park*
Starry, Starry Night Pieced Cotton Quilt 40" x 48"

Dream City Grid Basket 10-1/4" x 11" x 10"

har Wiss never plans a basket: "The forms just grow," she says. "They have a life of their own."

Wiss works in coiled basketry, a method that goes back further than ancient Egypt, preceding the discovery of basketweaving. Her materials, though, are not the reeds of riverbanks, but modern telephone wire or rush (the twisted kraft paper used for country chair seats.) The coil is variably thickened or thinned by splicing or unsplicing wires and stripping off the insulation to taper the connection. Wound tightly around the rush or wire is colored, waxed Irish linen thread. The linen used to be available in only ten colors; now there are 34, which sometimes makes it harder, says Wiss, to decide what to use. Like patchwork quilters who use every bit of scrap, Wiss uses every last leftover strand of thread.

Char
Wiss
WILMETTE

Central
Illinois

Central Illinois is the land of Lincoln, hallowed ground, from the log cabin of Lincoln's boyhood in Lerna to New Salem, where he spent the early part of his career. From Springfield to Quincy and to Decatur, the settings of Lincoln's years as a legislator and his debates with Stephen Douglas, the region is rich with historical sites. A day at the State Fair in Springfield will show how rich the region is in other ways, as well. The landscape of central and eastern Illinois was planed level and flat by the retreating glaciers of the last Ice Age, creating in their wake perhaps the most fertile agricultural soil anywhere on Earth. The sheer abundance of fields planted as far as the eye can see is staggering. From August through October, overflowing grain trucks shuttle back and forth between the grain elevators and the reapers in the fields. The region's many county fairs and harvest festivals come one right after another, the Sweet Corn Festival in Hoopeston, the Apple 'n Pork Festival in Clinton, and the Nauvoo Grape Festival, to name just a few. The town of Arcola has its Broom Corn Festival in August and in mid-May, a festival celebrating Raggedy Ann and Andy, whose creator, Johnny Gruelle, was born there. Arcola is also the center of Illinois Amish culture. Amish buggies are a common sight on the roads. The food and hospitality of the Amish and the furniture produced in their cabinet shops are justly famed. About an hour southeast of Arcola is Charleston and Eastern Illinois University. Its landmark German Gothic castle, the Old Main, rises like an architectural fantasy off the prairie. Just south of Charleston along the Embarras River is Fox Ridge State Park, a great place for fishing, boating, hiking, and camping. About an hour north is the cosmopolitan campus of the University of Illinois at Champaign–Urbana, whose Krannert Art Museum houses the best collection of sculpture and painting outside of Chicago.

Left
Redbud Trees at Kickapoo State Park, Oakwood

Barrie
Bredemeier
URBANA

T he glass artist Barrie Bredemeier and his wife, the sculptor Hyon Joo Kim, have a showroom next to their house on the outskirts of Urbana. The name, "Glass Lake Studio," is an homage to the eternally liquid nature of glass, molten or cooled. In the garden between the house and the studio is a pond full of bright orange koi swimming among lily pads—glass art come to life. Also in the garden is a pair of bronze life-castings of Bredemeier's hands holding one of his glass platters up to the sun. Bredemeier's work crosses a spectrum of techniques. Among his finest recent pieces are a series of ikebana vases with boatshaped cross-sections. A resourceful craftsman, Bredemeier often makes his own tools, like the wooden formers for cups and bowls immersed in buckets of water behind his glassblower's bench.

Above
Ikebana Vase Blown Glass 10-3/4" x 10" x 4-1/2"

Left
Water Bowl Blown Glass 9-1/2" x 12" x 12"

Top
Dana Thomas House Interior, Springfield

Bottom
Buffalo at Wildlife Prairie Park, Peoria

Right
Mississippi River near Delabar State Park, Oquawka

David Griffin

CHARLESTON

David Griffin's silver and enamel tea services push past traditional limits of form and function. Not content just to pour out cups of Sleepytime, Griffin's jumpy "Red Zinger Heater Meter," has an anodized aluminum handle cannibalized from a flashlight and caution stripes on the lid. "No Explanation Needed" ("Lift and Pour") pays homage to the Pop artist, Roy Lichtenstein. The green-enameled "Teatime in Texas," with yellow coil springs for handles, has silver wire drawings of a longhorn, barbed wire, and an oil well, connected to cutouts of Griffin's native state of Texas on the lids. "Tea Crane" makes witty use of the mechanisms of derricks and cranes. The tea infuser, suspended from a steel wire, can be reeled in and out with a little crank. A cluster of tiny organ pipe-like tubes makes up the spout.

Tea Crane Copper, Sterling Silver and Enamel 8" × 5" × 4"

Red Zinger Heater Meter Sterling Silver, Aluminum and Enamel 10" × 8" × 5"

Celeste
Lyon

Celeste Lyon takes the same pleasure in her work that a pastry chef takes with a cake. The charm of her gaily painted low-fired whiteware is that it is genuinely sweet, a flavor not easy to bring off without becoming cloying. The engobe glazes on Lyon's large, fanciful bowls, platters, and vases decorated with childlike images of flowers and animals are like icing drizzled over cakes. Her sunny and vivacious Caribbean palette radiates cheer out of everything she turns her hand to, from her inexpensive slip-cast garden ornaments—a ladybug, a tiny cup—and—saucer birdbath, a butterfly, and a little bird—to her elaborate garden fountains with pumps, to her endearing bird—and—flower—ornamented teacups which look like little girl tea-party teacups that have grown up unapologetically feminine and prim.

Composite Vase Clay 17" x 10"

Vessel Porcelain 14-1/2" x 12"

Ernest
Miller
CHAMPAIGN

rnest Miller explores the realm of crystal glazes on the smooth fine-grained surfaces of porcelain. What happens after a glaze is applied and a ceramic is consigned to the fires of the kiln is a mystery that can never be fully anticipated by science and method alone. In crystal glazes, the right temperature and flow of flame will induce the growth of crystals from metallic salts, producing blooms and discs of color, something like the way a pearl grows around a grain of sand. The form of the ceramic itself is also a factor: crystals form differently on a horizontal platter where the glaze pools than on an urn where the glaze runs down the sides. When Miller unbricks the door of the kiln after a firing, it is never with a sure idea of what lies inside, which is precisely what keeps this potter going.

Geometric Designs Ukranian Pysanky-Hen and Bantam Eggs

Mary Dilliner is self-taught in the meticulous art of Pysanky, or Ukrainian decorated eggs. Pysanky are not painted eggs but dyed, using a wax-resist process. With each successive color dyed, the egg's intricate design is increasingly concealed, the results more and more hidden till all the beeswax is melted off with a candle at the end. The best eggs for pysanky come from domesticated hens, bantams, ostriches (whose eggs weigh five pounds each) ducks, and geese. No two eggs, even laid by the same bird, ever come out the same—each one takes dye differently and there is no predicting how. Dilliner works freehand. She is devoted to the correct use of the old slavic folk-symbols and colors, all of which carry specific meanings whose qualities, it is believed, transfer to the person the egg is given to.

Mary
Dilliner
ARCOLA

Don Pilcher
CHAMPAIGN

More a sculptor than a potter in recent years, Don Pilcher was persuaded to return to making porcelain vessels when his wife said, "Look, I'm going to need something to remember you by when you're gone. At least make me the urn for your ashes." Pilcher's underlying forms are exceptionally graceful and pure, and might be called "classic" were he content to leave them looking "nice." Instead, he encrusts them with some of the imperfections of hard-won experience, disturbing the smoothness of the pristine forms with bits and lumps expressive of the truth of ordinary life. Coming straight from his subconscious, the impulse to work like this came to Pilcher one day when he began to marvel at the residue of things his kids left on their dinner plates, the ambiguous debris of vegetables and clumps of cappellini.

Ceramic Jar Porcelain 9-1/2" × 6" × 6"

Bill Heyduck, *Charleston*
3 Cat Jars Stoneware Ceramics 3-1/2" × 4"/5-1/2" × 6"/8" × 10"

Poppy Vincent, *Chatham*
Fantasy Flight 2000 Brooch, 18K Yellow Gold, Silver, Enamel, Boulder Opals, Peridot, Ruby, Green Tourmalines, and Iolites 3" × 4"

Cindy Romano, *Monmouth*
A Son's Coverlet Fiber 70" × 76"

Dwight Crane, *Rantoul*
Quake Woodworking 8" × 9"

51

Susan
Gorman

Susan Gorman's jewelry and ornaments have attracted the attention of such institutions as The DeBeers diamond consortium, The Smithsonian, and The White House, where, in 1993, Gorman's sterling silver and gold holly wreath was one of the ornaments selected for the White House Christmas Tree in celebration of the Year of American Craft. Gorman produces a new limited edition silver ornament every year. A ring by Gorman in sterling silver and tourmaline is part of the Smithsonian's permanent collection. Another of her rings won a prestigious DeBeers Diamonds of Distinction award. Gorman says, "Each colored stone has a personality all its own and must have its own space to proclaim itself, to allow it to be fiery or tranquil. The design of the mounting should follow the dictates of the stone."

Above
Granite & Diamond Brooch 14K Yellow Gold Jewelry 1-3/4"

Left
Sugilite, Pink Tourmaline, Pearl Earrings 14K Yellow Gold Jewelry 2-1/4" × 1/2"

Left
Lincoln's Home, Springfield

Above
Sculpture Garden at Allerton Park, Champaign

Victoria
Woollen–Danner

CHARLESTON

Enameling is a process in which colored glass in the form of powders, grains, millefiore and beads, glass-charged crayon or watercolor is applied to various metals, then fused to the metal in a kiln. Beyond the work she does with enamel in jewelry, Victoria Woollen-Danner explores the medium in framed works of assemblage. The journal she keeps of her dreams is the wellspring of her imagery. The enameled elements are painted with images of doors within doors, or an open window with curtains billowing against the sky, or—one of the most haunting—the ghost of her mother. Suspended from these images on brass or silver wires are charms and bits of memorabilia like the tip of the rib of a deer, a fluorite crystal (the state mineral of Illinois), and a poignant photo of Victoria's mother as a child.

Dieing Is a Wild Night and a New Road Vitreous Enamel, Copper, Acrylic Paint, Wood and Brass 13-1/2" x 8-3/4"

Doris
Knoblock

Doris Knoblock's majolica pottery is so animated that it seems to move. Pale yellow salamanders creep along the tops of teapots. Rays and squid swim ornamentally round the rims of bowls. Fat pink garden slugs crawl up the sides of vases. The creatures that come wriggling forth in clay from the jungles of Knoblock's imagination match the tales of her travels through Mexico, Guatemala, North Africa, Indonesia, Turkey, Greece, and the Far East. An animist on perpetual safari, she has hunted folk-art everywhere from Bali to Oaxaca to Istanbul. Deeply versed in the alchemy of iridescent lustres and glazes, Knoblock sometimes deliberates for days before deciding which colors she will use. Her textures and patterns are so complex that some of her animals require four or five separate firings in the kiln.

Above
Double Serpent Teapot Ceramic-clay and Glaze 15" x 10" x 10"

Right
Manta Ray Bowl Ceramic-clay and Glaze 18" x 18" x 5"

Billie Jean Theide, *Champaign*
Butte #EF-8 Teapot, Metal 4-3/4" x 12" x 2-1/2"

Bruce Nix, *Maroa*
Sugar Maple Natural Edge Bowl Woodworking 12" Diameter

Deb Ryman, *Springfield*
Ocean Goddess Jewelry/Hand-made Glass Beads 24" Long,
Mermaid 1/2" x 3"

Karenlee & Chuck
Spencer

CHARLESTON

The first plants cultivated by man were gourds. If matured on the vine, hard-shell gourds, unlike squash or pumpkins, will cure and stay hard forever. They are naturally occurring leakproof containers. Chuck and Karenlee Spencer call them "Nature's Tupperware." On a tree-shaded homestead at the end of a country road in Charleston, the Spencers have a cottage industry in growing and hand-painting hard-shell gourds. Karenlee makes over thirty different characters, including Santas, Angels, and one called the Herb Lady. Chuck's characters have eyes and mouths like jack-o'-lanterns. Besides cats and devils, his creatures include a guy called Eggplantheadman, a happy couple called Slimelime and Bittersweet, and the gaping Widemouth Jack, who wears a wonderfully shaped hat made from the top of the gourd.

Flower Lady Hardshell Gourd 10" Tall x 8" Diameter

Gourd Spirit Pot Hardshell Gourd and Deerskin 11" Diameter

Left
Lincoln Statue at Lincoln's New Salem
Historic Site, Petersburg

Above
Lincoln's New Salem State
Historic Site, Petersburg

Right
Sunrise Middle Fork of the Vermilion River
at Kickapoo State Park, Oakwood

The Ancient Cornplanters Ceramic 16-1/2" x 19"

David
Mott
C H A R L E S T O N

It's one thing to think about living in harmony with nature, another to spend your days doing it. The potter and bow-hunter David Mott considers all creatures—including the deer he hunts to supply his family meat—to be his brothers. "My religion tends to a kind of animism; it is related to the Native Americans' consciousness of man's place in and obligations to the whole of nature." Mott is a close student of the wildlife and archaeology of his Charleston habitat, where the landscape abruptly changes from the glaciated prairies of central Illinois to the forested hills of the south. Made from clay he mixes with his feet and glazed with ashes from the wood of his own trees, his platters, teapots, storage jars and reliquaries sensitively depict the animals and birds that live wild outside his door.

Grapeleaf & Vine Table Forged Steel 34" × 30"

The strapping great-granddaughter of a Danish coppersmith, Lorelei Sims has smithing in her blood. You can see from the 150 lb. powerhammer at her forge in Charleston that the woman means business. After taking degrees in sculpture and metalsmithing and apprenticing with an old North Carolina blacksmith, Sims opened her own forge in 1993. She produces both functional objects and delightful garden sculptures, the latter made of objects found at the local junkyard, which, to her, is a sort of paradise. Her work includes railings and garden gates, kitchen hooks and pot racks, coat trees, wine racks, candelabra, tables with glass tops over bases of forged grape leaves and grapevines hung with grapes made of balls of carbon steel, as well as lovely goddess icons for your garden.

Lorelei
Sims
CHARLESTON

63

Dwain Naragon

WESTFIELD

The vessels of Dwain Naragon would not look out of place balanced on the heads of women in the villages of Africa and India. Naragon is a teacher of clay and a prolific production potter. His interest is in the forms generated by tribal cultures, and their universality from one culture to the next. His work is richly informed by knowledge of ceramic history, making reference to forms as varied as Chinese ewers, Islamic vases, Greek amphorae, North African jugs and urns, the stupas of Buddhism, and the onion-domes of Russian churches. A craftsman with a clean, sure sense of design, Naragon's feeling for rhythms of pattern and form is amplified by his work in basketry, knitting, and crocheting, then expressed in clay by his rapidly incised, repeating patterns of feathers, chevron, lattices and grids.

Above
Bow to the Queen Stoneware 19-1/2" Tall

Left
Tribal Queen Stoneware 15" Tall

Far Left Top
Suspension Bridge over Mackinaw River at
Parklands Foundation Merwin Nature Conservancy, Eureka

Far Left Bottom
State Capitol Building, Springfield

65

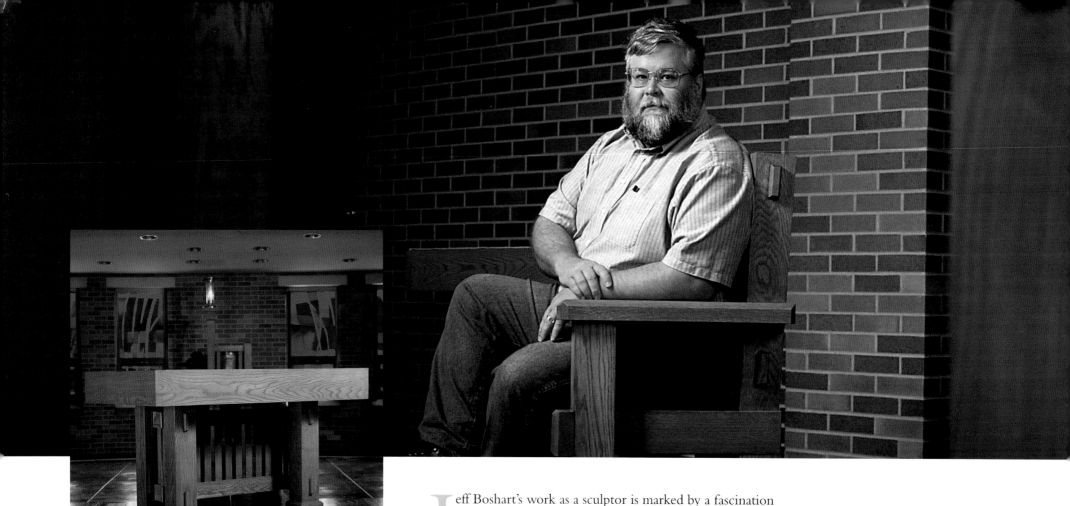

Altar, St. Philip Neri Chapel Newman Center Charleston, IL Oak 40" × 64" × 40"

J eff Boshart's work as a sculptor is marked by a fascination with the industrial engineering aesthetic of the 19th and early 20th centuries. A professor of art at Eastern Illinois University, Boshart is noted for his large constructs of heavy timbers and railroad ties on the theme of bridge and trestle structures. He is similarly drawn to the structural and functional clarity of Mission style furniture. That interest was intensified by his discovery in the Eastern Illinois University library of a complete leather-bound set of Gustav Stickley's pioneering magazine, *The Craftsman*. When offered the opportunity to create the liturgical furniture for the chapel of university's Catholic student center, Boshart responded with Mission designs in oak for the ambo, the altar, several side tables, a tabernacle tower, and a Pascal candle stand.

Jeff
Boshart
CHARLESTON

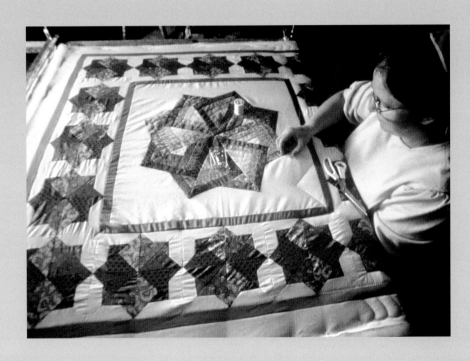

Above
Day Lilies at Lincoln's New Salem
State Historic Site, Petersburg

Left Top
Mennonite Quilting, Arthur/Arcola

Left Bottom
Spirit of Peoria on the Illinois River, Peoria

Large Brass Bowl Raised Brass 6" x 12"

Joe
Spoon

CHARLESTON

J oe Spoon's name really is Joe Spoon and he truly does make spoons. His catalog of brass kitchen utensils includes ladles, skimmers, serving forks, sets of measuring spoons and cups, bowls, colanders and pothooks. The alloys and the silver solder used for the joints are lead-free and food-safe. Spoon also makes candlesticks, candelabras and menorahs, ceremonial cups, plant hangers, fireplace tools, birdbaths, hardware for garden gates, and cabinet drawer-pulls. He forms his fluid, serpentine handles by heating brass or bronze rod with a torch to a dead-soft cherry-red and working it freehand. The highly polished bowls, cups, and the round bellies of the spoons are initially formed by hammering sheet brass into hemispherical hollows carved into the top of stumps of elm logged from Spoon's own woods.

Cast Bracelet Sterling Silver 2-1/2" x 2" x 1-1/4"

Beverly
Fagan
URBANA

Beverly Fagan likes to keep her jewelry simple. She works in gold, sterling silver, semi-precious stones like onyx, carnelians and lapis lazuli, and pearls as well, but her aim is not to create hugely expensive museum pieces. She would rather make her jewelry accessible to the people who visit her booth at art shows and crafts fairs around Illinois, many of whom are return customers. Her designs include cast, forged, and fabricated gold wedding rings, gold and silver earrings, and silver collars or chokers with slides. One of her most popular designs is an earring that looks like a pair of calipers measuring the diameter of a small sphere of silver or gold. On her forged chokers and earrings, Fagan has achieved a linear texture in silver that shimmers like water spilling over a fall.

Rimas VisGirda, *Champaign*
Two Cups - Teapot Ceramics 9" x 10" x 5-1/2"

Charlie Sweitzer, *Champaign*
Shaker Rocker Woodworking 41" x 19" x 17"

Tanya Shur, *Champaign*
Boy with Bird Ceramic Tile 5" x 5"

William
Carlson
URBANA

The granite and glass interfaces of the sculptures William Carlson is internationally known for are laminated to each other with enormous technical skill, leaving no perceptible flaws in the joints. The clarity and openness of the glass is encased in the absolute opacity of stone. Their displaced but highly controlled fault-lines grind against each other at the edge of chaos, like tectonic plates. Carlson's more recent works, wall-hung groupings of square tiles of clear glass cast with the textures of things like corrugated cardboard and bubble wrap, are a radical departure from his familiar hardedged constructivism. The tiles are first sandblasted and stained with oxides, then partially polished back so that you can make out fragments of Latin imprinted on the backsides, utterances of a vanished tongue.

Quadrant Construct, 2000 Granite, Glass and Steel
27" x 26" x 14-1/2"

71

Southern
Illinois

Southern Illinois sits at the edge of the state across the Ohio River from the state of Kentucky. The further south you go, the slower the pace of speech, the softer the accents, and the more places you find that serve grits. Removed from the speed and hustle of Chicago, southern Illinois is conducive to both creation and recreation. Many artisans have homesteaded in the region to start cottage industries in pottery, blacksmithing, glass, and fiber. Artists at Southern Illinois University in Carbondale and Edwardsville continue the crafts revival they initiated in the sixties. Within an hour of Carbondale are some of the most beautiful scenic areas of Illinois. Don't miss the astonishing cubic rock formations in Giant City State Park, with accommodations at the massive WPA-built stone and timber Giant City Lodge and cabins nearby. The Lodge is an excellent base for excursions into the surrounding region, certainly for a wine tasting and picnic at one of the many local and award-winning vineyards or a visit to the artisans' boardwalk in the tiny town of Makanda, just a few minutes away. Makanda is a gateway to the Shawnee National Forest, a favorite destination for backpackers and hikers. About an hour northeast is the famed Rend Lake Resort and wildlife area, and the Illinois Artisans Shop at Rend Lake, which exhibits and sells works by many of the artisans featured in this book. Two hours northwest of the Big Muddy River and Carbondale is the Collinsville-Edwardsville area (only twenty minutes east of St. Louis). Here you'll find one of the largest vestiges of ancient civilization in North America, the Cahokia Mounds, a United Nations World Heritage Sight. A few minutes beyond is the monument commemorating Lewis and Clark's point of departure for their expedition to the West. Not far away is the handsome river town of Alton, whose suspension bridge, one of the most beautiful of any span across the Mississippi, is a sight not to be missed.

Left
Rock Outcrop at Pounds Hollow in Shawnee National Forest, Vienna

The work of the Makanda cabinetmaker Kyle Kinser was honored in 1997 with a show at the Illinois State Art Museum. Kinser works mostly in native timbers, primarily walnut and cherry logged from the woods of southern Illinois. He and his sons often plank the logs themselves, keeping the boards in sequence and making it possible to build a piece or a set of furniture from matched pieces of the wood of a single tree. The fine proportions, exposed joinery and hand-planed surfaces of Kinser's furniture exhibit his respect for the work of two great elders of American woodworking, James Krenov and George Nakashima. Drawing from the simplicity and clarity of the Shaker style and the aesthetic of tansu, the traditional storage furniture of Japan, Kinser is creating an elegant new Midwestern idiom of his own.

Kyle
Kinser
MAKANDA

75

Top Left
Bicycling Along the Great River Road at
Pere Marquette State Park, Grafton

Bottom Left
Vandalia Statehouse State Historic Site, Vandalia

Above
Bald Cypress Trees at Heron Pond
Cache River State Natural Area, Belknap

Brent
Kington

MAKANDA

Brent Kington has the classical craftsman's respect for the demands of function, and feels a responsibility to answer to it in his sculpture, whose only function is to radiate beauty. His works of forged steel revisit ancient forms—the Axis Mundi, or the spear planted in the ground to claim one's place, the crescent shape, the horns of the bull in the Greek myth of Europa. Exquisitely balanced above and rooted to the ground below in bases of oak or maple shaped with tools Kington has forged himself, his works possess the dignity of a tribe of silent, radiant beings. They speak a wordless language of their own. Trained as a silversmith, self-taught as a blacksmith, Kington founded the blacksmithing program at Southern Illinois University. A smith of smiths, he has forged not only steel, but a generation of smiths to follow.

Crescent Hot Forged Carbon Steel and Oak 91" x 10" x 10"

Crescent Hot Forged Carbon Steel and Oak 59" x 16" x 11"

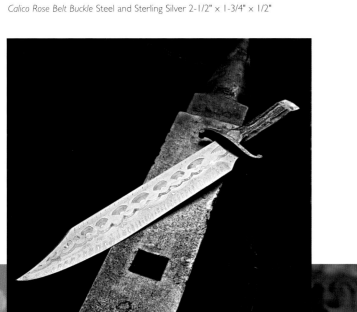

aryl Meier is a master of Damascus steel, or "pattern welding," a technique whereby many thin layers of contrasting types and colors of steel are forged together with a massive powerhammer. The patterns formed in the metal resemble topological maps, or watered silk, or figured maple. A 1/4" thick blank for a knife blade can consist of 240 or more paper-thin layers of steel, each only 1/1000" thick. A blank can be reforged and folded back upon itself to form ever more complex layers of patterns, which are further emphasized by treatment with acids that etch and color each type of steel to different effect. Meier's Damascus steel blanks are coveted by jewelers, gunsmiths, and knifemakers. Former Governor James R. Thompson made a gift of one of Meier's Bowie knives to former President George H. Bush.

Daryl Meier

C A R B O N D A L E

Left
Stream in Bell Smith Springs at Shawnee National Forest, Vienna

Above
Pierre Menard Home State Historic Site, Ellis Grove

Untitled Suppressed Volume with Two Triangles Porcelain 16" × 14" × 4"

Ceramicist Harris Deller's square porcelain plates, or "wall platters," are formed by pressing clay into a "hammock mold," a square wood frame the bottom of which is fabric. The frame is then raised off the worktable, allowing the wet clay to slump and take the form of the sagging fabric. Surfaces are then incised with grids or patterns like the parallel whorls of a person's thumbprints, or the sinuous combed lines of Japanese raked gravel gardens, and the engraved lines fired with black glaze. Vessels such as the masklike "Untitled Suppressed Volume with Two Triangles," are first formed on the potter's wheel, then taken off the wheel and shaped so their sides press towards each other. Their outlines evoke the shapes of the ceremonial jade axes Deller has seen in his travels to Korea, China, and Japan.

Harris
Deller
CARBONDALE

81

"In one of a life's rare moments of complete clarity, within the first instant of striking hot metal with a hammer, I knew what I wanted to do in life…the connection for me between sculpture and smithing." John Medwedeff has now been smithing for twenty years, the last few of them in a steel building his wife says "looks like a giant toaster." He bought the building from a shut-down coal mine on a bleak, rainy November afternoon in 1996, then reassembled it on the site where it now stands. His first large commission here was the fountain for the square of his town of Murphysboro. The sinuous curves of his sculptures flow from the world of Art Nouveau: "No one becomes a blacksmith today who isn't a romantic—but I'm a forward-looking romantic; technology expands the range of what is possible for me to do."

John
Medwedeff
MURPHYSBORO

Darby
Ortolano
MURPHYSBORO

nlike the materials of other crafts, clay has little inherent aesthetic appeal as a raw material. " We're talking mud here," says Darby Ortolano, but it is just that--the primal aspect of clay--that makes Ortolano want to get her hands into it. She has played with many different kinds, from stoneware to porcelain to the earthenware she's been doing recently. Called "majolica" (painted, low-fired red terra-cotta, the familiar clay of flower pots) her earthenware speaks of sunshine, the Mediterranean, and a cheerful love of life. In one group, a pitcher and four cups called "Summer Garden," the colors are so vivid you can almost smell the flowers. The cups are fuller at the bottom, narrowing at the top like old-fashioned milk bottles. They fit the hand, and nestled against the pitcher, look right too.

Ginkgo Leaf Platter & Sugar/Creamer Set Majolica Glazed Earthenware
22" Platter/11" Wide Set

Alpha Omega Silver 23" x 11"

F amed for their intricate precision and complexity, the chalices of the silversmith Richard Mawdsley have been exhibited in museums all over the world. His "Alpha and Omega," a standing cup of solid sterling silver with gold and rhodium plated elements and pearls mounted on a mahogany base, is the fifth of a series based on the water towers of small Midwestern towns. Mawdsley worked on this piece over a period of five years. Its details depict objects that left impressions on him growing up in Kansas in the 50s—the air-raid sirens that fed the fear of nuclear destruction and that today still warn of the dread approach of tornadoes, the charred remains of a bombed-out church, the street lights that pierce the rural darkness with eerie, isolated cones of light. The closer you scrutinize Mawdsley's work, the more worlds it reveals.

Richard
Mawdsley
CARTERVILLE

85

Barbara Niechciol & David Parrish, *Cobden*
Untitled Artist Etched Jewelry 5/8" x 1-1/2"

Rory Jaros, *Cobden*
Walden Rocker Wood 42" x 26" x 36"

Sandstone Formations Overlooking Garden of the Gods, Shawnee National Forest, Vienna

Mary M. Pizzini, *Edwardsville*
Maori Sunset Acrylic Sculpture 31" x 21" x 5"

Roberta Elliott, *Cobden*
Table Lamp Hand-forged Steel and Blown Glass 30" x 20" x 20"

M. Joan
Lintault
CARBONDALE

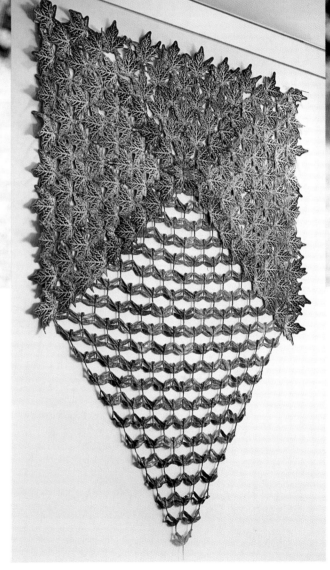

Flight Path 100% Cotton Fabric 10' × 10'

Breathtaking in size, in the intensity of their color and detail, and in the sheer quantity of patience and love that go into them, Joan Lintault's internationally celebrated quilts fairly teem and spill over with life. Her quilts come close to being biological phenomena. To grow one, Lintault starts with lengths of unbleached cotton muslin and her own handmixed dyes and paints. She prepares about 15 yards of fabric at a time, laying it on the ground in her back yard and simply throwing the dye on it. She then meticulously cuts, quilts, paints and otherwise embellishes the myriad details, layering them with so much wit and substance that you have to peer deep into the quilt for it all to register. A woman of endearing candor, when asked what she calls the open spaces of her quilts, she says, "Holes."

Aphrodite 192 Carat Australian Opal Carving, Set in 14K and 18K Gold with 19 Emeralds 1-1/2" x 5"

The goldsmith Allan Stuck makes wearable objects of jewelry—rings, pendants, brooches, and the like—but prefers to call himself a sculptor. Stuck works with very old pieces of the world. His work is informed by a lifelong interest in paleontology, geology, biology and botany, all evident in the sinuous lines of his gold mounts for precious stones and his use of organic materials—shark teeth, bear claws, mother of pearl, and perhaps most astonishing, fragments of the agatized or petrified bones of dinosaurs. One material, called ammonite—the petrified remains of the shell of a huge prehistoric snail—has the dazzling properties of a kaleidoscope, with gorgeous flakes of bleeding crimson, flashing greens, blues, fiery oranges. Stuck's shop is right across the railroad tracks from the Boardwalk in Makanda.

Allan
Stuck
MAKANDA

Part of Daniel Johnson's bucolic 15 acre farmstead in the peach-orchard country of Alto Pass is planted with a forest of oak, tulip poplar, sassafras, and white pine. Paths meander through the woods past Johnson's sculptures of steel and concrete. Other sculptures, some over 20 feet tall, stand out in the open fields. Some are for sale, others inspire commissions for new works. From his small "sketches" in steel to large works in colored cast concrete, Johnson's sculptures often recount stories through words and pictograms embossed or cut into their surfaces. His family experiments with "collaborative collage"—people suggest shapes for Johnson to cut and weld—led last year to "Cotton Candy Couldn't Be Any Tastier," a sculpture created with the input of visitors to the Illinois State Fair at Du Quoin.

Daniel
Johnson
ALTO PASS

Far Left Top
Giant City State Park Lodge, Makanda

Far Left Bottom
Native American Indian Youth at Cahokia Mounds
State Historic Site, Collinsville

Left
Sunset at Garden of the Gods Wilderness Area,
Shawnee National Forest, Vienna

Right
Stone Stairway at Bell Smith Springs
in Shawnee National Forest, McCormick

Above
Twilight at Horseshoe Lake Conservation Area, Granite City

Frye
Tim & Pam
SHUMWAY

Tim and Pam Frye's Pottery is a cottage industry whose success hinges on skill, consistency, and speed, all necessary to making attractive work by hand that people can afford. The couple does sixteen crafts fairs each year. Every piece of their stoneware is a collaboration. Pam makes most of the the smaller objects—sets of cups, small bowls, and the like. She also does all the brushwork, swiftly and deftly laying down such motifs as bluebirds, dragonflies, lilies, and stalks of wheat. Tim does most of the larger pieces like pitchers, tureens, and salad bowls. But whether it's butter trays, garlic crocks, or teapots, both touch every piece at some point in the process. "This work is soothing," says Tim. "You reach a state of calm from the repetition. You get into it and after a while, it's like a dance."

Tea Set Stoneware 10" Tall

Paper Cuts (Tea Pot) White Earthenware Treated with Stains, Slibs, and Glazes 28" x 26" x 15"

The ceramic artist Annelies Heijnen often works barefooted, and as you can see from her work, with all the exuberance of someone stamping grapes. Her low-fired glazed earthenware ranges in size from ordinary scale to teapots so big it would take two people to lift one of them and pour. Heijnen is as much a sculptor and painter as she is a potter. The boldly colored surfaces of her platters, bowls, teapots, and large freestanding and wall-hung tableaux swarm with life. Both the inside and outside surfaces of the work teem with watchful cosmic eyes and droll, enigmatic images of people, birds, flowers, serpents, bugs, and trees, all wide-eyed and astonished at the fact that they exist. Heijnen's studio is in Mt. Vernon, not far from the Illinois Artisans Shop at Rend Lake, where her works are on display.

Annelies
Heijnen
MT. VERNON

Zoe Godby Lightfoot, *Marion*
Morning Glory Pool Pendant and Neck Ring Jewelry Printed, Patinated, Sterling Silver
with Chrysophraese Cabochon 5" Diameter

Tiford & Sue Hord, *Beecher City*
Small Bucket White Oak, Hickory, and Walnut 7" Tall x 10" Diameter

Information Available Upon Request

Ché
Rhodes
CARBONDALE

Musing on the nature of glass in both its molten and solidified states, Ché Rhodes observes, "The glass remembers everything you do. It is a record of its own handling, of moments of hesitation, however slight, of the pauses in its manipulation as it cools and thickens. As soon as you remove glass from the melting furnace, you are essentially freezing its action into form." Director of the studio glass program at Southern Illinois University, Rhodes works mostly in clear untinted glass. His art combines a fascination with the physics, mechanics, and optical qualities of glass with radical exploration and experimentation in a material that is idiosyncratic and unpredictable in its behavior. He embeds polarizing filters in some work, for example, to give internal expression to the stress patterns imparted to the glass as it froze.

Paul Dresang

EDWARDSVILLE

Paul Dresang deplores contemporary civilization's impoverishment of the sense of touch. His deliriously erotic trompe l'oeil porcelain teapots sit in "unzipped" burnished "leather" bags complete with metallicized ceramic snaps, rivets, buckles, and "brass" zippers. They would give anyone who was to touch them plenty to think about. In contrast to Dresang's funny, obsessively detailed "teabags" are his far less ambiguous straightforward works of functional stoneware pottery. Regardless of the mode he's working in, Dresang's concern is always for balance—of color, qualities of warmth and coolness, sensuousness and texture. "Soul is the heart of the matter," he says, and his works have it, counteracting what he calls "the emotional deficit" of so many of the uninspired industrial objects we live with.

Above
Untitled Porcelain 18" × 16" × 16" Detail

Far Left Top
Geese on a Southern Illinois Pond

Far Left Bottom
Downtown Makanda

Left
Untitled Porcelain 18" × 16" × 16"

Southern Illinois Woodland Mask Mixed Media, Fibers, Silk Ribbon, Antique Braid, Glass Beads, Peacock Feathers, Pheasant Feathers, Reeds, and Brass
26" × 8" × 22"

The powerful animal spirits embodied in the masks of American Indian, African and other ancient cultures are the inspiration for the dramatic ceremonial headdresses and masks of fiber artist Marilyn Codding Boysen. Intricately constructed fantasies, her masks endow the wearer with the spirits they depict—the shy grow bold, the meek ferocious, the homely, beautiful. Boysen works in an amazing profusion of materials: reeds, sticks, seed pods, thorns, and electroplated leaves as well as semi-precious stones, pearls, brass, silver, ribbons, braid, myriad buttons and smashed rusted bottle caps, bits of leather, snakeskin, and the feathers of roosters, turkeys, pheasants, parrots and the lone peacock that struts about the farm that she and her husband, glass artist Bill Boysen, share in Cobden, southwest of Carbondale.

Marilyn
Codding Boysen
C O B D E N

S educed though he is by "the sensuousness of glass…its surfaces, its color," Bill Boysen likes to play with finishes that contradict its native voluptuousness. His work challenges the conventional utility of glass containers. He embeds forests of tacks, for example, upon the outer surfaces of his bowls, and makes vessels that instead of resting upon a stable foot, roll tilted on their sides. Boysen founded the studio glass program at Southern Illinois University in the late sixties. Now retired, he still loves going on the road with his "Aunt Gladys," the mobile studio he created at Southern Illinois University, to give demonstrations of the art of glassblowing to rapt audiences at fairs and museums all over the Midwest. He and his wife, the maskmaker Marilyn Boysen, live in a converted chicken coop on their farm in Cobden, southwest of Carbondale.

Bill Boysen
COBDEN

Ceremonial Vessel Blown Glass, Mixed Media 10-1/2" x 11" Diameter

Handwoven Rug Fiber 38" x 63"

Anita
Hayden

MAKANDA

Anita Hayden weaves rugs on a 90-year-old loom that she bought from her sister who got it from an old blind weaver in Murphysboro. She works with everything from textile mill discards like sock tops—the loops trimmed off socks before the top is elasticized—to scrap fleece from sweatshirt factories. Cotton sheets, worn blue jeans, corduroy pants, even fine chenille bedspreads rescued from motels past their prime, all find their way to her loom. Ms. Hayden's loom is set up right in her shop, Southern Sisters, on the Boardwalk of the village of Makanda, outside Carbondale. She can create a rug of any size up to 40 inches wide to 20 feet long and will do custom weavings of any size, matched to color samples. All her rugs are washable: the best way is to hang them on a clothesline and spray them with a hose.

Mourning Flower Vase Pewter and Aluminum 8" × 1-3/8" × 3-3/8"

For Paulette Myers, jewelry as sculptural objects and hollowware as sculptural form are vehicles for an intense exploration of the physical and spiritual properties of metals and precious stones. Her interest in the behavior of different alloys is as much scientific as artistic. She experiments fearlessly, working with gold, reticulated silver, copper, brass, bronze, pewter, titanium, niobium, and other materials even more exotic. Like a physicist, she inquires into their malleability, strength, and chemical interactions when heated, cooled, or subjected to pressure. Each pure metal or alloy has its own working qualities and fitness to particular designs. Their relationships become more complex with Myers' introduction into her compositions of carefully selected, spiritually charged amethysts, garnets, tourmalines, lapis, and rubies.

Paulette
Myers

E D W A R D S V I L L E

Art
Towata
ALTON

E ven the simplest container has to hold something besides dust. There should be something in it that makes others want to touch it, hold it, use it. Does it have life, movement, energy? Does the pot speak? Does it give you warmth, does it convey the time of the year, the time of the day, the season of its making, its youth or its age? Turning the pot in your hand, how does the view change…is it alive all around…?" Art Towata has been asking these questions of himself for fifty years. Fired with ash, his pots emerge from the kiln in families of similar form, but no two are the same. "Some are female in spirit, some male, some old as late winter, some young as new bamboo. Because they are fired at extremely high temperatures, if you tap them or run a finger around the rims, they ring, and the rims sing."

Top
Untitled Stoneware Jar 30" × 11"

Left
Family of Jars Stoneware 4"-5" Tall

Above
Pair of Radiator Cans Wood-fired and Soda-fired Stoneware, Decals and Metal Wire 16" × 18" × 10"

Far Left
Garden of the Gods in Shawnee National Forest, Vienna

Left
Pair of Oil Cans Wood-fired Stoneware and Decals 30" × 18" × 8", 12" × 10" × 5"

Dan Anderson's work in clay is based on a collection of old funky beat-up oil, gas, and kerosene cans found at farm auctions and antique and second-hand stores. Poignant with nostalgia for a rural world in decay, Anderson's trompe l'oeil, corrugated stoneware surfaces simulate the rusted, dented, weatherbeaten look of old metal and barnsiding. Some of them bear faded traces of the decals and signs the petroleum companies used on their cans and the sides of barns back in a time shiny with industrial optimism. Anderson is similarly obsessed with the forms of water towers, "the Sphinxes" of his youth in the Midwest. The ancient look of his glazes is the result of wood-firing at high temperatures in the anagama, or tunnel kiln Anderson built behind his house with the help of his students.

Dan
Anderson
E D W A R D S V I L L E

Trellis Handmade Paper 41" × 46"

Like confetti flung into the air, the torn paper collages of Connie Miller are acts of spontaneity and joy. Not nearly as easy an effect to achieve as it might appear, the exhilaration Miller makes visible comes from an ordered sense of design. With simple, torn pieces of colored paper, Miller creates a lyric alphabet all her own and writes with it with pleasure. Each work starts with paper made by hand from the purest bleached cotton fiber. Luxuriating in color, Miller saturates the paper with colorfast cold-water dyes. Once the color is set, she tears the paper carefully by hand. The strips are then pressed into the composition, again by hand, not with a press. Her works look as though made of layers of richly colored felt, or the petals of fresh flowers, or stained glass, inexplicably lit from within.

Connie
Miller

EDWARDSVILLE

Artisan Index

T he Illinois Department of Commerce and Community Affairs hopes that this book will inspire you to call and visit the artists, the Artisan Shops and other galleries which represent them. There is nothing like seeing works of the quality shown on these pages in person. Visits to the regions where our artisans live and work will reward you with both the finest crafts of Illinois and greatly satisfying experiences of the state's many natural, cultural, and vacation wonders along the way. We warmly encourage you to call, pack up the car, and explore.

ILLINOIS STATE MUSEUM – ILLINOIS ARTISAN SHOPS

The Illinois Artisans Program, administered by the Illinois State Museum, promotes the rich heritage of fine crafting in Illinois and markets crafts through artisans shops in Chicago, Springfield, Lewistown, and at Rend Lake

Illinois Artisans Shop
James R. Thompson Center
100 West Randolph Street
Suite 2-200
Chicago, IL
312. 814. 5321
Mon-Fri 9 - 5

Illinois State Museum -
The Museum Store
Spring & Edwards Street
Springfield, IL 62706
217. 782. 0979
Mon-Sat 8:30 - 5
Sun 12 - 5

Southern Illinois Artisans Shop
and Visitors Center
I-57, just west of Exit 77 (Rend Lake)
Whittington, IL 62897
618. 629. 2220
Open 7 days a week 9 - 5

Dickson Mounds Museum Gift Shop
10956 N. Dickson Mounds Road
Lewistown, IL 61542
309. 547. 3721
Daily 8:30 - 5

PARTICIPATING ILLINOIS AGENCIES

Illinois State Museum -
Illinois Artisans Programs
James R. Thompson Center
100 West Randolph Street
Suite 4-300
Chicago, IL 60601
312. 814. 4945 312. 814. 1794
fax: 312. 814. 2439

Illinois Arts Council
James R. Thompson Center
100 West Randolph Street
Suite 10-500
Chicago, IL 60601
312. 814. 6750
fax 312. 814. 1471

TRAVEL INFORMATION

For travel information about any of the sites featured in this book, please call 1-800-2CONNECT or search online at www.enjoyillinois.com
TTY: 1-800-406-6418

A–C

Dan Anderson
Edwardsville
618. 656. 7775
Priced: $1,500 - $3, 000

Angarola
Vernon Hills
312. 405. 0255
Priced: $5,400 - $12,000

Allison Ashby & Steve Jedd
Riverside
708. 185. 5116
Priced: $1,000 - $34,000

Alan Barbick
Warrenville
630. 393. 1615
Priced: $5 - $4,000

Jeff Boshart
Charleston
217. 345. 5882
Priced: $2,000 - $6,000

Bill Boysen
Cobden
618. 893. 2962
Priced: $500 - $3,500

Marilyn Codding Boysen
Cobden
618. 893. 2962
Priced: $500 - $12,000

Barrie Bredemeier
Urbana
217. 328. 0589
Priced: $300 - $750

William Carlson
Urbana
217. 328. 6636
Priced: $18,000 - $20,000

Dwight Crane
Rantoul
217. 893. 4610
Priced: $8 - $1,200

D–F

Harris Deller
Carbondale
618. 549. 5460
Priced: $800 - $3,000

Michael Devlin
Chicago
773. 235. 5517
Priced: Upon Request

Mary Dilliner
Arcola
217. 268. 4407
Priced: $75 - $100

Paul Dresang
Edwardsville
618. 656. 2480
Priced: $8,000 - $10,000

Central

Southern

Map not shown to scale.

ARTISAN INDEX

Roberta Elliott
Cobden
618. 893. 2216
Priced: $5 - $1,500

Paul Eshelman
Elizabeth
815. 858. 2327
Priced: $65 - $100

Beverly Fagan
Urbana
217. 367. 9546
Priced: $30 - $500

Mark Fowler
Rock Island
309. 788. 2081
Priced: Upon Request

Susan Etcoff Fraerman
Highland Park
847. 831. 0356
Priced: $1,800 - $10,000

Michele A. Friedman
Chicago
773. 465. 3901
Priced: $30 - $360

Tim & Pam Frye
Shumway
217. 868. 5583
Priced: $12 - $200

G-H

Robert Gadomski
Homewood
708. 957. 4875
Priced: $250 - $9,000

Susan Gorman
Champaign
217. 356. 5466
Priced: $100 - $1,000

David Griffin
Charleston
217. 348. 0779
Priced: $600 - $1,200

Paula Grill
Wilmington
815. 773. 4680
Priced: $105 - $185

Anita Hayden
Makanda
618. 457. 8508
Priced: $68 - $72

Annelies Heijnen
Mt. Vernon
618. 242. 9092
Priced: $1,500 - $2,400

Bill Heyduck
Charleston
217. 345. 7325
Priced: $15 - $50

Tiford & Sue Hord
Beecher City
618. 487. 5726
Priced: Upon Request

Dorothy Hughes
Chicago
312. 421. 7045
Priced: $4,800 - $12,000

I-K

Rory Jaros
Cobden
618. 893. 4639
Priced: $350 - $2,500

Daniel Johnson
Alto Pass
618. 893. 2894
Priced: $10 - $10,000

Indira Freitas Johnson
Evanston
847. 475. 6192
Priced: $1,000 - $10,000

Adair Karlin
Highland Park
847. 831. 2917
Priced: $50 - $450

Akiko Koiso
Rock Island
309. 793. 4660
Priced: $450 - $1,000

Marcia Karlin
Lincolnshire
847. 940. 4930
Priced: $800 - $4,000

D. Andrew Kates
North Aurora
630. 482. 3808
Priced: $100 - $10,000

Brent Kington
Makanda
618. 549. 7926
Priced: $5,000 - $12,000

Kyle Kinser
Makanda
618. 549. 4540
Chicago
773. 248. 6067
Priced: $50 - $12,000

Doris Knoblock
Heyworth
309. 473. 3590
Priced: $500 - $1,500

Richard Kowal
Chicago
773. 929. 3028
Priced: $30 - $300

L-N

Zoe Godby Lightfoot
Marion
618. 964. 1121
Priced: $10 - $450

M. Joan Lintault
Carbondale
618. 457. 5460
Priced: Upon Request

Joyce P. Lopez
Chicago
312. 243. 5033
Priced: $3,000 - $150,000

Celeste Lyon
Springfield
217. 546. 8030
Priced: $275 - $500

Lisa Mahar
Rock Island
309. 786. 4397
Priced: $100 - $350

Richard Mawdsley
Carterville
618. 985. 4705
Priced: $300 - $40,000

John Medwedeff
Murphysboro
618. 687. 4304
Priced: $3,000 - $50,000

Daryl Meier
Carbondale
618. 549. 3234
$250 - $75,000

Connie Miller
Edwardsville
618. 659. 1622
Priced: Upon Request

Ernest Miller
Champaign
612. 821. 8270
Priced: $250 - $500

David Mott
Charleston
217. 345. 5780
Priced: $150 - $500

Paulette Myers
Edwardsville
618. 345. 6300
Priced: $1,000 - $2,000

Dwain Naragon
Westfield
217. 967. 5373
Priced: $85 - $2,500

Barbara Niechciol
& David Parrish
Cobden
618. 893. 1505
Priced: $15 - $25

Bruce Nix
Maroa
217. 794. 5774
Priced: $10 - up

O-Q

Mary Carolyn Obodzinski
Crystal Lake
814. 477. 2455
Priced: $50 - $500

Darby Ortolano
Murphysboro
618. 687. 9231
Priced: $50 - $300

Karen Ovington
Chicago
773. 764. 5200
Priced: Upon Request

Ana Buzancic Petercic
Lincolnwood
Priced: $250 - $350

ARTISAN INDEX

Bonnie Peterson
Elmhurst
630. 782. 5530
Priced: $500 - $10,000

Don Pilcher
Champaign
217. 367. 8821
Priced: $300 - $1,000

Mary M. Pizzini
Edwardsville
618. 656. 0662
Priced: Upon Request

R–T

Weeks Ringle & Bill Kerr
Oak Park
708. 445. 1817
Priced: $100 - $6,000

Ché Rhodes
Carbondale
618. 457. 1605
Priced: Upon Request

Lori Roderick
Rock Island
618. 788. 2081
Priced: $250 - $850

Cindy Romano
Monmouth
309. 734. 2913
Priced: $2 - $1,500

Deb Ryman
Springfield
217. 544. 9338
Priced: $38 - $100

Vera Samycia
Chicago
773. 792. 3329
Priced: $25 - $75

Jane A. Sassaman
Chicago
773. 248. 3659
Priced: $1,000 - $2,000

Marvin & Michelle Shafer
Chicago
773. 525. 3729
Priced: $25 - $2,000

Deborah Shank
Northbrook
847. 272. 5831
Priced: $200 - $250

Tanya Shur
Champaign
217. 355. 6152
Priced: $10 - $100

Doris Sikorsky
Chicago
773. 631. 3811
Priced: $200 - $2,000

Lorelei Sims
Charleston
217. 345. 1159
Priced: $1,200 - $2,200

Robert Sjostrom
Rockford
815. 965. 7574
Priced: $25 - $130

Karenlee & Chuck Spencer
Charleston
217. 345. 4389
Priced: $75 - $300 and up

Joe Spoon
Charleston
217. 348. 1657
Priced: $50 - $300

Robert Stewart
Cary
847. 639. 3017
Priced: $3,000 - $16,000

Kurt Strobach
Crystal Lake
815. 459. 7377
Priced: $130 - $400

Allan Stuck
Makanda
618. 529. 2341
Priced: $500 - $50,000

Charlie Sweitzer
Champaign
217. 352. 1618
Priced: $30 - $500

R. Thomas Tedrowe Jr.
Chicago
312. 492. 8316
Priced: $975 - $20,000

Billie Jean Theide
Champaign
217. 398. 1956
Priced: $2,000 - $5,000

Art Towata
Alton
618. 462. 5926
Priced: $75 - $3,000

U–Z

Elaine Unzicker
Chicago
773. 907. 8401
Priced: $100 - $400

Poppy Vincent
Chatham
217. 483. 2156
Priced: $20 - $40,000

Rimas VisGirda
Champaign
217. 398. 1956
Priced: $500 - $1,500

Laura Wasilowski
Elgin
847. 931. 7684
Priced: $100 - $3,000

Mary Watson
Prospect Heights
847. 253. 5806
Priced: $50 - $500

Spencer Watson
Prospect Heights
847. 253. 5806
Priced: $25 - $150

Ruth Weiner
Evanston
847. 328. 5558
Priced: $850 - $2,500

Jennifer Forman Weinstein
Chicago
toll-free 866. 240. 0247
Priced: $85 - $250

Kathleen Weir-West
Barrington
847. 438. 1130
Priced: $450 - $1,500

George Weissler
Evanston
847. 475. 7783
Priced: $350 - $1,200

Leonard & Carolyn Wilson
McHenry
815. 459. 5849
Priced: $8 - $145

Char Wiss
Wilmette
847. 256. 5664
Priced: $1,000 - $1,100

Karla Witukiewicz
Chicago
773. 489. 3924
Priced: $250 - $500

Victoria Woollen-Danner
Charleston
217. 348. 5974
Priced: $40 - $800

Larry Zgoda
Chicago
773. 483. 3970
Priced: $80 - $6,000